CU00405377

The Experience of Grace

Aspects of the Faith and Spirituality
of the Puritans

David Sceats

Director of Local Ministry and Principal of the LNSM Scheme
in the Diocese of Lichfield

GROVE BOOKS LIMITED
RIDLEY HALL RD CAMBRIDGE CB3 9HU

Contents

The Cover Illustration is by Peter Ashton

Copyright © David Sceats 1997

First Impression August 1997
ISSN 0262-799X
ISBN 1 85174 352 9

The Hotter Sort of Protestants

Perceptions of Puritanism

Puritanism has had a chequered past. From the outset the world gave it a bad press. The steward Malvolio, in Shakespeare's *Twelfth Night*, is a case in point, displaying already, as the sixteenth century became the seventeenth, the characteristics that were to become its stereotype—humourlessness, prating hypocrisy, self-righteousness, the tendency to take oneself far too seriously, spiritual pride and snobbery. Puritans themselves did not always help their own case. Take the names they gave themselves, for instance: the 'Barebones Parliament' of 1653 was named for one of its members, Praise-God Barbon, a name that sounds outlandish enough to modern ears. At the time it was relatively restrained, however; according to the eighteenth century biographer James Granger, Praise-God had a brother, If-Christ-had-not-died-thou-hadst-been-damned Barbon![1] Such outlandish extremism seems to confirm the impression that, in Puritanism, we are dealing with an embarrassing and unsavoury manifestation of religious loss of proportion.

There is another side to the coin, however. Ever since the seventeenth century there have been Christians who looked back to the Puritans, not just as a source of inspiration, but as a motherlode in which to mine the raw materials of practical theology, pastoral ministry, good practice in homiletics, and spiritual psychology. Rediscovery of the writings of the Puritans was one of the keys that set loose the eighteenth-century evangelical revival. The impressive uniform sets of 'Complete' and 'Select Works' that issued from publishing houses like Nicholls of Edinburgh and Nisbet of London in the nineteenth century are testimony to the continued fascination that Puritanism exercised over the Victorian mind. And the reprints of Puritan sermons and treatises that the Banner of Truth Trust published at subsidized prices in the 1960s and 70s demonstrate how the fascination can still exert power within certain versions of evangelical spirituality today.

The Puritan Mindset

What is it about Puritanism that some Christians find so compellingly attractive? Well, for a start, Puritans were enthusiasts for reform. It was, as

---

1   J Granger, *Biographical History of England*, (1769) iii, 68. Inevitably, non-puritans generally referred to Praise-God's brother as 'Damned Barbon'! He is sometimes identified with Nicholas Barbon, who introduced the underwriting of fire insurance to the City of London. The impression that 'Damned Barbon' traded under the name of Nicholas reinforces the appearance of hypocrisy, though *The Dictionary of National Biography* is sceptical about the identification!

one Elizabethan pamphleteer economically put it, 'the hotter sort of Protestants' who were called Puritans.[2] The movement began among those in the reign of Elizabeth I who agreed with William Fuller that

'but halflie by your Majesty hath God bene honoured, his church reformed and established, his people taught and comforted, his enemies rejected and subdued, and his lawbreakers punished.'[3]

Puritanism, in other words, began as a reform movement, or rather as a movement of those committed to pushing to its logical conclusion the programme of reform in the English Church initiated in the time of King Edward VI, but interrupted by Queen Mary's reign of terror. Puritans were thoroughgoing adherents of the reforming programme. What distinguished them was (in Patrick Collinson's words) 'everything that separated real from merely formal Protestants,'[4] and it is in this enthusiasm for reform that one of the secrets of their attraction to subsequent generations lies. The totality of their commitment attracts as much as it repels, challenging us especially at a time when passionate intensity is under suspicion. Half measures would never be enough for the true Puritan. It was middle ways, judicious balancing acts, attempts to hold together conflicting positions, that would always be suspect—tinged with compromise and betrayal.

What is significant about this totalitarian commitment to reform, however, is the way in which it displays how, in a very real sense, Puritanism was a theologically conservative movement. The Puritan psychology manifested an essentially scholastic approach to religious questions and, like most scholasticism, it was not entirely free from the marks of what, today, has come to be described as fundamentalism. Puritans found themselves constrained by the momentum of the inner logic of their system to press everything to its ultimate conclusion. This could (and, by the 1640s, increasingly did) degenerate into fanaticism, but amongst the leaders of mainstream Puritanism within the national church (both lay and ordained) it was coupled with a commitment to scholarship and academic rigour, and this meant that it expressed itself as a kind of intellectual passion—a passion whose roots lay in the theology of John Calvin, specifically in the form taught by his successor at Geneva, Theodore Beza.

It could well be argued that Bezan Calvinism was the last great wing of the edifice of mediaeval scholasticism. Its use as the conceptual bedrock of Puritanism meant that the theological resources the Puritan divines brought to their project of nurturing a thoroughgoing pattern of Christian discipleship emphasized deductive argument, logic (the practical syllogism was one

2   Percival Wiburn, *A Checke or Reproofe of M Howlett's Untimely Screeching* (1581).
3   William Fuller, *A Booke to the Queene* (Unpublished MS, c1593).
4   P Collinson, *The Elizabethan Puritan Movement* (Jonathan Cape, 1967).

of their favourite homiletic devices), authority, rhetoric and tradition. All grace, as they understood it, was mediated through the understanding. The thinking mind was the crucial human faculty in the things of God:

'"God opened the heart of Lydia." The heart is put for the whole soul. He opened her understanding to conceive; for all things begin with the heavenly light of the understanding. All grace comes into the soul by the understanding.'[5]

Yet at the same time they stood for 'a feeling religion' and the validity of what they described as 'practical, affectionate divinity' (that is, a theology of human experience), and this serves to illustrate a deep fault-line which runs right through the foundations of their spirituality. For if Beza's version of Calvinism was a Protestant scholasticism, then it was also the intellectual antithesis of the humanism out of which Calvin's own thinking had grown, and that strand of Calvinism had its own part to play in the construction of the Puritan mindset. It contained the seeds of a political radicalism that would, eventually, bring down the English crown. This radical tendency in Puritanism can be traced back to the discovery of the individual which began with Renaissance humanism and was baptized by the Protestant Reformation. Individualism led Puritans to an emphasis on private judgment in religion, to a concern with the Christian man and his relationship with God (Puritans were not much troubled by our notions of political correctness, though they had a version of their own), to value the religious experience of individuals, especially in relation to conversion and grace and hence to explore the psychology of Christian experience. It led them to emphasize the nurture of the individual soul and the provision of a pattern of pastoral support whose model was the essentially individualistic work of the physician.

Much of Puritanism (especially of Puritan spirituality) can only be understood if the inner conflict between these two tendencies, the conservative and the radical, is grasped. While, intellectually, Puritanism was conservative, even reactionary, psychologically and politically it was radical, and, eventually, revolutionary. This tension ran right through Puritanism, affecting its spiritual, political, and theological agendas and leaving its leaders constantly wrestling with the problem of providing theologically conservative interpretations of religious experience which would emphasize the dominance of the understanding over the affections, with tools that encouraged politically and spiritually radical perceptions about the significance of individual experience and conviction.

It is not our purpose here to define Puritanism, or even to offer a simple

---

5   Richard Sibbes, 'Lydia's Conversion,' *The Riches of Mercie* (1738) in *Works* (1863) vol VI, p 523.

yardstick by which we could determine whether a given individual 'deserves' the name. It was, at the time, a defamatory term; it is only in later ages that it has come to be used by some as a badge of honour. Richard Baxter describes how his father was jeered at for being a Puritan because he read the Bible aloud with his household each Sunday.[6] Seventeenth century people did not usually apply the term to themselves; they were much more likely to talk about 'the godly' or 'the saints and people of God.' It was as much a move-ment within the established church as outside it, until the very end of its period (the mid-1640s onwards); many of its leading figures were willing if not enthusiastic participants in an episcopally ordered church.[7]

But if we cannot define Puritanism, we can characterize it, and the best way to do this is the way the Puritans themselves would have done—by telling a story. Early on in the Puritan period the adherents of the movement were described in a number of ways—'Scripture men,' 'such as run to hear preaching,' for instance—but their commonest nickname was 'precesians.' They were 'precise,' not only in their religious practices, but also in their daily lives and behaviour. The story concerns Richard Rogers, vicar of Dry Drayton near Cambridge in the late sixteenth century, who was out riding in his Fenland parish one day when he chanced upon a neighbouring Gentle-man with whom he fell into conversation. As they were about to part, his companion said something to the effect that he had greatly enjoyed Rogers' company, 'but I must ask you sir, why are you so precise?' 'Oh sir,' said Rogers, 'I serve a precise God.' That, in a nutshell, says a great deal about the spirit of English Puritanism.

It should be clear by now that what distinguishes Puritanism from other expressions of Protestantism was (and is) its psychology, or spirituality, not its particular belief system. Indeed, in the late sixteenth and early seven-teenth century, virtually all English Protestants would have subscribed the same set of doctrinal beliefs. At the Hampton Court Conference in 1604, when the leaders of the Puritan movement met with James VI of Scotland and I of England, one of the major Puritan demands was for the inclusion of Arch-bishop Whitgift's Lambeth Articles in the 39 Articles of the Church of Eng-land, on the grounds of their theological congeniality to the Puritan party. Whitgift had been no friend to Puritans! Later, it is true, opposition to Puritan-ism came to be identified with the Arminianism of William Laud and his school, and this creates an impression that the conflict was essentially be-tween Calvinists and those opposed to 'the religion of Geneva.' But this is to misunderstand what was essentially distinctive about Puritanism, which was its particular religious psychology, that is, its pattern of spirituality.

6   N H Keeble (ed), *The Autobiography of Richard Baxter* (1974), (abridged by J M Lloyd Thomas from *Reliquiae Baxterianae*, 1696) p 6.
7   For example, William Perkins, Richard Rogers, Richard Sibbes.

Protestant Totalitarianism

That spirituality can, perhaps, best be described as Protestant totalitarianism. For instance, one manifestation of what it meant for Puritans to be 'precise' was the dissolution, both implicit and explicit, of the divide between the sacred and the secular. This is an idea with which we are familiar, though in a rather different sense from that in which a Puritan would have intended it. The form that such a denial most often takes in our own times is marked by scepticism about the plausibility of the religious standpoint. Human life is the overarching category; religious affiliation is seen merely as one (not especially verifiable) aspect of it. It is what certain people choose to do for a sense of meaning. For Puritans, by contrast, life was an aspect of the greater, all embracing category of religion. Man's chief end was to glorify God and any other proximate ends that got in the way of this ultimate one must be ruthlessly excised.

It is here, perhaps, that the influence of Calvin on Puritanism was most strongly felt. The Puritan religious psychology began from a deep pessimism about human nature—what was most evident about people was their sinfulness, by which Puritans meant not so much the particular acts of evil that people performed as the underlying corruption or distortion of human nature that was their effective cause. The roots of the Puritan preoccupation with saving grace and conversion that we are about to explore lie here in the tension between human depravity and human destiny, man's sin and man's chief end. And the link between the two was the providential rule of God.

Writers on Puritanism have sometimes supposed that, because they were Calvinists, the doctrine of election lay at the heart of their theology and spirituality. This probably represents as much a misunderstanding of Calvinism as of Puritanism. Puritans did, of course, believe in predestination, in most cases in the austere Bezan form of the doctrine known as double predestination,[8] in which the decree of predestination is held to be logically prior to those of creation and redemption, and in which, therefore, it is hard to escape the conclusion that the reprobate perish, not so much because of their sin as because of their reprobation, while the elect have no choice in the matter of their good works and ultimate salvation. But it is not necessary to read very widely in Puritanism to recognize that its followers were not principally concerned (as some writers have suggested[9]) with the question of whether or not they were elect. The decree of election was secret; it belonged to 'the hidden things that are known only to the Lord our God'[10] not to the things that are revealed, which 'belong to us and to our children.' What concerned Puritans was not what they could not know, but what they could.

---

8 See, for instance, the Chart of Election and reprobation in W Perkins, 'A Golden Chaine,' *Works I* (1608) p 9.
9 eg W Haller, *The Rise of Puritanism* (Harper, 1957) pp 83ff.
10 Deut 29.29.

What was available to them in the way of knowledge was whether or not their lives and experience showed evidence of the gracious operation of God's Spirit. The question for the Puritan, therefore, was not 'Am I elect?' but 'Am I manifesting the marks of grace?' or 'Where can I see the signs of the Holy Spirit at work in me?'

Providence

This concern for evidences of grace is simply one manifestation of the overarching Puritan concern with the idea of the Providence of God. Puritan totalitarianism included the assertion that the sovereignty of God was total. His rule was necessarily to be seen as much in the circumstances of daily human life as it was in the hidden questions of eternal destiny. Predestination and providence were, indeed, two parts of the same piece, for what the saints were elect to was salvation, and salvation was only attainable through faith. Faith was the human religious affection that answered to the grace of God—only through the gracious operation of God's Spirit could one exercise truly saving faith, and the evidence that one was, indeed, a recipient of grace was that one's life was characterized by godly works. Election and grace belonged in the hidden realm of the divine decrees. But faith and good deeds were very much part of the visible realm in which God ruled through the operation of his providence. It was through God's providential disposing of an individual's circumstances, therefore, that he or she would encounter the means of grace, come to faith, and exercise those godly works which were evidence of truly gracious affections.

God's sovereignty in providence was as complete as his sovereignty in grace. In effect, every circumstance of life, even the seemingly most trivial, was suffused with latent religious significance. The choice of a pair of boots whose toes pinched might seem to have nothing to do with God and his grace, but if it caused the traveller to rest for a moment at the crossroads at just the moment when a godly neighbour was passing by on the other road, and they fell into a conversation about the things of God which led the traveller to attend to the means of grace, it could be seen to have been part of the providential rulings of the 'precise' God. Because of the chain of efficient causality, all circumstances interlocked in this way, and therefore none was without its latent religious significance even if, in the vast majority of cases, the significance never emerged. In effect this was the application of Protestant scholasticism to human circumstances. Just as, in the theoretical system of scholasticism, every issue in the end comes to bear the same weight, because the whole edifice stands or falls by the logic of its inner coherence, so it is with human circumstances. Every event, however small, is potentially as significant as the great event of all, since all are interconnected by the chain of efficient causality. All events are, therefore, potential evidences of God's providential rule and care.

A Feeling Religion

Words and the Word

You have only to look at their writings to see that words were the medium of communication with which Puritan divines felt most comfortable. This should not surprise us. They spoke and wrote the language of Shakespeare with all its energy, vigour and colour. They lived at a time of unprecedented creativity and productivity in English letters, when communications technology was organized around the printed page and when books, though costly, were still enough of a novelty to have something of the impact that the Internet has today. But there are deeper reasons, too, for their preoccupation with words. In part it reflects their belief that the means by which grace influences human beings is the understanding or rational mind. If all grace is mediated through the understanding, by which is meant the conscious mind of perception, thought, analysis and reflection, then language is crucial, and verbal media of communication are paramount. But behind this perception of how human beings participate in the gracious operations of the Spirit lies a conviction about how God has communicated with us.

When Puritans spoke about 'the Word' they most often meant not the incarnate Lord Jesus Christ but the text of Scripture. In the seventeenth century all Protestants accepted that the Bible was divinely inspired and, therefore, had a unique authority for the church and the believer, and Puritans, therefore, seldom found themselves in dispute with others over the nature of Scripture. Differences did arise, however, over the question of the practical limits of biblical authority. It was agreed by all that the Bible contains both positive commands and negative prohibitions, but the point at issue was the area of 'things indifferent' between the two. In this area, might the church use its own authority to make rules, or should the individual Christian have scope for liberty of conscience and self determination? The heart of the Puritan dispute with the 'Anglican' establishment was over the claim made by the bishops that in this grey area the church (by which, of course, the bishops meant the government) had power to determine and enforce rules of conduct and procedure. Against this view Puritans asserted a regulative principle of biblical authority, in which the Scriptures provided an exhaustive set of prescriptive rules for church and believer beyond which the church had no authority to insist on anything that was not explicitly insisted on by the Bible, nor prohibit anything that was not so prohibited.

This sounds like rigid fundamentalism. But in practice it had the opposite effect, as can be seen from the way in which Puritans were always demanding liberty of conscience. While it might look as though the regulative principle should have led to a pattern of church life which replicated the culture and circumstances of the first-century Roman Empire, it was, in practice, saved from such a fate by two hermeneutical devices. The first of these was the concept of the right of private judgment which, in effect opened an important door to the importation of human reasoning into the interpretation of Scripture. The second was the principle of rational extension—that the regulatively 'explicit' teachings of the Bible included 'what may be proved thereby.' These two devices allowed for the inclusion of considerable flexibility into the way the Scriptures were actually interpreted, while retaining the outward appearance of a single biblical authority. In effect, therefore, Puritans (who subscribed to the prescriptive regulative principle) were left with greater freedom than Anglicans (who rejected it in favour of a more normative view of biblical authority).

In the light of the place the Bible occupied in the Puritan scheme of things, it is not surprising that the primary means of grace for all Puritans were the Scriptures and the sermon, with the catechetical dialogue a close runner-up. Not surprisingly also, most Puritans felt uncomfortable with non-verbal (and especially non-verbalizable) forms of religious experience. Psalm-singing might be acceptable, since the music was a vehicle for the words and enabled everyone to join in together, and it was possible to believe that the words were what was 'really' communicating, but 'pure' music was distinctly questionable. So too was 'pure' silence—if space was not filled with words, it should be filled with thoughts, and the more verbal the better. Dance was, of course, unthinkable as a religious exercise, though there is evidence that some Puritans allowed it some value as a physical recreation.

It is easy, however, to misunderstand Puritanism at this point, particularly when we read Puritan texts today. Approaching its literature from a post-modern world of sound-bites, instant tell, visual images on TV and video, and contemporary fiction it is easy to suppose that people in the seventeenth century had the same difficulty with these weighty tomes as we do. Of course they did not, or these books would not have been published. There must have been a market for them in order for it to have been worth their publishers' while to go to the expense of producing them. Books were not cheap in the early 1600s! And once we break through the barrier of archaic spellings and Shakespearean syntax, the reason for their popularity becomes clear. For despite their appearance, these are not fusty academic tomes filled with 'cold' intellectualism. They are vigorous, earthy texts, full of stories and imagistic, even tabloid, illustrations. This is popular literature, and its writers prided themselves on the fact that they were communicating in ways which were immediately accessible to all, even the least educated.

The fact is that the vast bulk of these texts were sermons before ever they were books—indeed, many of them are simply volumes of sermons taken down virtually verbatim. They suffer some of the inevitable consequences, of course—repetition, digression, rhetorical flourishes that work in the pulpit but not on the page. But they bring us to the very heart of the genius of Puritanism, because what they are all concerned with in one way or another is helping ordinary people to have a 'feeling religion.' Their titles give the game away: *A Lifting up for the Downcast*; *Precious Remedies Against Satan's Devices*; *The Bruised Reed and Smoking Flax*; *Heaven on Earth*. Because of their conviction about the understanding as the gateway of the soul, Puritan divines knew they had to use words to move people to faith. Inevitably, therefore, in the circumstances of their time, preaching was their most typical means of communication, and the sermon their characteristic art form. But their aim in preaching was to go beyond merely offering propositions for the consideration of their hearers, or stringing together verbal felicities. This was the sort of preaching which was widely respected outside Puritan circles. It was characteristic of places where educated people gathered—royal chapels, cathedrals, universities, the Inns of Court. The Puritans rejected and despised it. However clever and 'witty' it might be, they saw it as designed simply to display the person and talents of the preacher. They wanted to preach in such a way as to enter the hearts and souls of their hearers. They would do so through the understanding, but their aim was to engage the affections, stir the emotions and, in the end, to move the whole person to response. The claim that all grace was mediated through the understanding, therefore, must be carefully understood. It did not mean that the effect of grace was *restricted* to the understanding—indeed, much to the contrary. Puritan divines wanted people to have a feeling religion, and their sermons were carefully constructed to that end.

Practical Divinity

It is significant in this connection that Puritanism never produced a systematic theologian. John Owen, the great Congregational divine of the Commonwealth came closest to it,[11] but he was a polemical and occasional theologian, not a real systematizer. William Perkins, recently described to me by an American colleague as 'the main man' of both North American and English Puritans, wrote a great doctrinal treatise,[12] but the bulk of his three huge folio volumes of *Workes* is made up of pastoral theology and sermons. In this, as in so much else, Perkins set the tone for those who would follow, and, at the same time, illustrates something distinctively English about Puritanism—that it was never overly impressed with the purely theoretical. The phrase the Puritans themselves used to describe their theology was 'practical affectionate divinity,' and they prided themselves that, as the name suggests, it was a theology that engaged with—indeed, arose from—experience,

---

11 For example, J Owen, *The Death of Death in the Death of Christ* (1647); *Pneumatologia, or A Discourse Concerning the Holy Spirit* (1674).
1 2 W Perkins, 'A Golden Chaine,' *Works I* (1608) pp 9-118.

context and situation, seeing itself as the handmaid of godliness.[13] In this it was directed and informed by the Puritan pattern of spirituality, rather than *vice versa*; the reason for studying theology was to understand and promote the logic that lay behind the practice of godliness. Puritans would hardly have acknowledged the notion of 'pure theology' and would have been distinctly uncomfortable with the idea that theology might have been studied as an academic discipline without reference to its situational application. Illustrative of this is a text that would have been on virtually every Puritan bookshelf, William Ames' *Conscience, with the Power and Cases Thereof*, a compendium precisely of situations analysed and explored in terms of how the godly man should act with spiritual and theological integrity. This contextual and situational aspect to Puritan divinity gives it a peculiarly contemporary ring. Of course the situations described, the language used, and the solutions proposed belong to the cultural and historical context of the seventeenth century, but the underlying assumptions about the nature of theology as an essentially practical and contextual discipline, and its link to human experience, may suggest another reason for the continuing interest which Puritanism attracts, especially at the present time.

One effect of this emphasis on practical affectionate divinity was that, for all their scholasticism, Puritan divines tended to begin with the 'facts' of spiritual experience, and seek their explanation in terms of the logic of the Calvinistic system they had received, rather than starting with the system and trying to fit the facts into it.[14] This could and did lead to disagreement, both about aspects of the system itself[15] and about matters of practical divinity, such as the nature of saving faith and assurance, and the relationship of the Christian believer to law and duty. It also meant, more interestingly, that Puritan divines often emphasized human responsibility far more than they are credited for. Indeed, because of their tendency to start from experience and always to take account of it in framing theology, some Puritan statements on subjects like using the means of grace and preparing for the gracious operations of the Spirit, if taken out of context, could easily seem to be teaching salvation by works. Such perceptions challenge the common stereotypes of Puritans as doctrinaire fatalists teaching 'the grim religion of Geneva,' or as pharisaical tyrants proclaiming a 'gospel' of law, duty and obedience without the balancing emphases of grace and forgiveness.

---

1 3 The word 'affectionate' is used in this phrase to connote 'concerning or in relation to the affections,' ie the subjective, non-cognitive, affective aspects of human identity, in short—the feelings.

14 Thus, in arguing that puritanism must be understood as an attempt to fit spiritual experience into the logic of predestination, W Haller, *The Rise of Puritanism* (Harper, 1957) misunderstands the essential nature of puritan practical divinity.

1 5 For instance, William Perkins followed the high calvinism of Beza on the order of the divine decrees of predestination, creation and redemption, whereas the Westminster Assembly adopted an infralapsarian position (predestination follows fall) in its Shorter Catechism.

We have considered already two of the three focal *loci* of practical divinity: the sovereignty of God and the depravity of humankind. The first had implications for the experience of both grace and providence, leaving Puritans with an essentially affirmative theology of circumstances. The second had a particular contribution to make to the way the experience of the work of God's Spirit was understood, for, as Puritanism saw it, the concomitant of depravity was our total inability to good, and consequent total dependence on grace. Grace was, therefore, the datum of salvation, in the light of which every aspect of the experience of the Spirit must be seen. Exhortations to repentance, preparations for the Spirit, the use of means, the call to faith, all must be seen only *within* the context of the conviction that without the operation of grace no spiritual movement was possible. Thus grace must always be understood as the conceptual context of Puritan preaching, and this would have been part of the shared but unspoken perceptual framework of both preachers and hearers, even when the sermon was about works of godliness. But human depravity had a second implication which significantly helped to shape Puritan spirituality. It led to scepticism about human institutions and activities unless they were redeemed by grace, and this could lead to either of two conflicting positions. On the one hand was the conviction that the world belonged to the saints, for only they could get its true flavour and benefit; on the other, it could lead to a denunciation of anything in the world that was not obviously a means of grace, a kind of Manichaeism that was more characteristic of some of the radical sectaries of the end of the Puritan period than of 'main-line' Puritan divines. In either case, however, Puritans were likely to value human institutions and activities, and the environmental world of non-rational creatures, simply as a means to gracious living[16] rather than for any intrinsic worth it might be deemed to possess.

The third major *locus* of Puritan practical theology was the necessity of the Spirit, and it is here that their dependence on mediaeval scholasticism is particularly apparent. Puritans followed Thomas Aquinas in a tendency to see grace as a divine infusion into human nature rather than as a relationship between God and man, and this sometimes reflects a failure to distinguish grace from the Holy Spirit, particularly as the Spirit's role is perceived as indwelling the believer. Nevertheless, Puritanism can only be understood as a religion of the Spirit, in which the Spirit was seen as an agent of all religious experience: regeneration, conversion, sanctification, assurance and perseverance. But as is so often the way in religions of the Spirit, Puritanism was most ready to part company with itself over questions of the Spirit's role in the work of grace in individuals and the church, and, in particular over the testimony of the Spirit to the gracious state of those who were the subjects of the Spirit's operations.

16 That is, the life of grace, not the life-style of the better-off!

13

3

The Means of Grace

The Lever of the Understanding

Puritans were always using means. If grace was mediated by the Spirit through the understanding, and if the understanding worked through processes of rational thought and reflection, then using means to receive grace was inevitable. Indeed, the ordinary way in which the Spirit would work would be by means. The understanding must have something to reflect on, and anything on which it might reflect which could lead to gracious influences on the affections, or to godly actions, was a means of grace. In principle, therefore, anything might be a means of grace, if it led the rational mind to faith and obedience. It was not that Puritans denied that the Spirit might work immediately, but they were convinced that the Scriptures presented both the Spirit and the human beings on whom the Spirit acted as rational beings, and that working by means was in fundamental accord with the character of the created order and with man's place within it. Since human beings were not self-existent but contingent, the ordinary mode of the Spirit's operations must also be contingent—by means.

But the Spirit was not tied to the means in any mechanical sense. Merely to use the means did not guarantee their end, for human beings were fallen creatures, and their depravity affected their reason as well as their moral character. There was a significant inconsistency here for Puritan spiritual directors for, according to their way of thinking, human reason was actually incapable of making proper use of the means of grace and since only proper use of the means could secure their end, human beings were effectively closed off from experiencing the gracious work of the Spirit. Only if a renewal of the human spirit took place as the Holy Spirit brought about the miracle of the new birth could anyone make proper use of the means, so that unregenerate 'hypocrites' who attempted to use them would fail to receive their benefits. But while this guarded effectively against a mechanistic, coin-in-the-slot view of the way the means of grace worked, it left an uncomfortable question about the new birth, since, in Puritan thinking, this, too, was a gracious operation of the Spirit through the understanding, and must, therefore, be brought about by means.

This raised several difficulties. For a start, how could the unregenerate 'enquirer' who wanted to discover faith be enabled to do so? The only way was to recommend the use of means, but proper use of the means was impossible before the reception of the gift of the new birth! More perplexingly, how, on Puritan premises, could an unregenerate 'enquirer' genuinely want to discover faith in the first place? If truly unregenerate, and therefore still in a state of depravity, not yet subject to the gracious operations of the Spirit, how could anyone experience a desire (for grace) which so palpably depended on having already experienced the mystery of regeneration? It was questions such as these that led to the Puritan fascination with the whole question of conversion and rebirth, and resulted in what was, in effect, the first serious spiritual psychology in English.

From the subjective point of view the effects of the new birth would be seen in terms of its effect on the rational faculties. It would give people the ability to recognize and accept their own dependence upon the means of grace for a genuine encounter with God's Spirit, and so to submit to God's sovereignty in providence and grace by making use of the means God had appointed. 'Hypocrites' could not get so far, for though they might use their rational faculties to understand 'from the outside' how the means might work, they would always be self-deceived in their attempts to experience their application. In practice, therefore, 'enquirers' were simply dealt with. They were exhorted to the right use of the means, in the confidence that only those in whom the work of grace had already begun would be capable of making such a right use, while doing so would have the effect of bringing the work of regeneration to full effect. Any hypocrites who tried to use the means, however, would fail, since they were not subject to the gracious operation of the Spirit. The Puritan divine did not need to know in advance who was a child of grace (which was just as well because, as we have already seen, this knowledge belonged to God alone); he merely needed to recommend people apply themselves to the means of grace. The outcome would disclose all.

The Nature of Grace

We have already noted the Puritan tendency not to distinguish clearly between grace and the Spirit of God. Another way of putting this is to say that Puritans tended to see grace as an influencing power or infusion in the heart. Joseph Symonds' description of the means gives the game away:

'There is a nutritive vertue in every ordinance; they are means appointed by God as pipes for the conveyance of living waters into those empty cisterns of our hearts; if therefore, either out of watchlessenesse, or pride, any doe withdraw from them, they withdraw from God.'[17]

The concrete imagery of water-pipes is a characteristic Puritan metaphor, but behind it lies an equally concrete perception of the meaning of grace, which represents a development in a mechanistic direction from the view of the sixteenth-century reformers, who tended to see grace in more relational terms as divine favour. This is significant. The reformers were protesting

17 Joseph Symonds, *The Deserted Christian's Case and Cure* (1639) p 153.

15

against the late mediaeval catholic tendency to see grace in concrete terms, which expressed itself in issues such as the sale of indulgences. In that context they naturally emphasized the source of grace in the unmerited favour of God. Puritans, on the other hand, were theologians of the spiritual life, whose primary concern was the spiritual experience of individuals. For them the issue was how grace was received, and it is not surprising that their understanding of it should be more concretized. At the same time, it is worth noting that this is not the only point at which Puritanism has more in common with late mediaeval catholic spirituality than with its own Protestant antecedents. There is a similarity of tone and moral value between the late mediaeval spirituality and Puritanism, and the essentially conservative character of much Puritan thought is also significant in this connection. Of course, the Puritan tendency to concretize grace can be over-pressed. Most Puritan writers were aware of the dangers of an impersonal conception of grace:

'...we may use the means, but there is no means under heaven will do it [ie, obtain grace]. Yet you must wait upon God in the use of the means, for it is not the means that will do it, that will work faith, but the Spirit of God in the use of means.'[18]

But despite such explicit rejections of the identification of grace and Spirit, the tendency to see grace in concrete terms as an infusion remained prevalent, and it is not hard to see how it is implicit in the kind of thinking about means that we have been considering.

Ordinances and Exercises

Since everything in life fell under the providential rule of God, any circumstance could, potentially, become a means of grace for the Puritan by affording an opportunity for spiritual reflection. In practice, however, Puritan divines found it helpful to 'classify' means of grace according to an ascending hierarchical scale. At the bottom were the natural and political providences of everyday life which only became means of grace for their subjects at certain times of what we would probably call coincidence and they described as providential ordering. Above these were the private means of grace or 'spiritual exercises'—prayer, meditation, Sabbath observance, Bible reading, self-discipline. Though these had the essential nature of means of grace they were undertaken privately, and some were not commanded of necessity by God. At the top of the hierarchy were the public means of grace or 'ordinances' (so called because they were ordained of God), the sacraments, public worship, catechizing, and, above all, preaching. The terminology was not fixed, however; 'ordinance' was capable of expansion to include

18 Thomas Hooker, *The Poor Doubting Christian* (1629) p 176.

any intentional meeting of the church, while 'exercise' sometimes referred to corporate activities, which could include preaching.[19]

Preaching was far and away the chief of the ordinances for all Puritans, and the reason for this is clear. In the context of the time it was the rational means of communication *par excellence*, the means most admirably suited to the mediation of grace to the person through the understanding. But it would be wrong to infer that the Puritan concern for rational communication was the same thing as an interest in intellectualism for its own sake. In fact Puritans, as we have already observed, eschewed the kind of intellectualism that marked much of the accepted technique of preaching in their day in favour of a new hermeneutical and homiletic theory. In a context in which many clergy did not preach at all, and sermons were seen as intellectual exercises for the intelligentsia, the Puritans' commitment to preaching as the chief means of grace led them to a homiletic that was 'plain' and 'painful.' Looking at their printed sermons today, we may feel that the adjective 'painful' was well chosen! What they meant by it, of course, was not what we mean. In the seventeenth century 'painful' meant 'full of pains,' 'painstaking.' It emphasized that the sermon was a matter for the investment of the major portion of the preacher's time and energy during its preparation—that sermons were not to be taken lightly as entertainments, but seriously as the key that might unlock the way to eternal life, and that their content should be shaped, not by the display of erudition for the greater glory of the preacher, but by a commitment to 'doctrine' and 'use.'

Doctrine and use were the twin poles of the Puritan homiletic technique. They arose from the conviction that the Spirit worked by means, and that therefore the sermon needed to be as well fitted as possible to bringing the understanding of the hearers into vital contact with the meaning of the word *for them*. 'Doctrine' meant simply the teaching of the Scriptures and 'use' its application to the hearers. In order to elucidate the first, Puritan preachers insisted on a rational hermeneutic based on the obvious sense of the words of Scripture in their biblical context, while to achieve the second they cultivated the unornamented but vivid and imagistic style we have already noted. Preaching remained, to be sure, a technical matter, but the techniques the Puritan preacher was concerned with were those of grasping the imagination of his hearers and leading them to 'use' the doctrine of the sermon for themselves. Obscurity was the cardinal sin, for it muffled the means of grace and interfered in the free play of the Spirit on the understandings of the people. The clearer the sermon the more effective the means, and the more likely it was to achieve its end.

---

19 Examples of this latter usage were the so-called 'Prophesyings' in the time of Elizabeth I, and the similar Cripplegate Morning Exercises of the 1640s.

4
Conversion—The Experience of Grace

The Christendom Context

Puritans were in no doubt about the necessity of conversion. It was the correlative of human depravity—human beings simply could not live for God without it. But this consensus still left a number of questions unanswered, most of which raised explicit or implicit issues about the psychology of Christian experience and its relationship to systematic Calvinism. Where did the experience of conversion fit into the complete work of grace? What were the distinguishing marks of conversion, and how could true conversion be distinguished from false? What was the relationship between conversion and saving faith? Was faith a precondition or a consequence of conversion? What constituted saving faith? What was the relationship between conversion and the ordinances, especially baptism?

These questions arose in a context with which it is hard for modern Christians, especially evangelicals, to identify. It was one of substantially universal church membership; in consequence there is very little evidence in the writings of Puritans of our common contemporary equation between conversion and 'becoming a Christian.' In the sixteenth and seventeenth centuries virtually everyone in England was a member of the visible church and therefore, at least implicitly, a professing Christian. Occasionally, especially towards the end of the Puritan period, the term 'Christian' can be found used in the sense of 'true believer,' but even then it usually has a qualifying adjective of some sort.[20] But earlier on this usage is virtually unknown; conversion was not the way in which someone became a Christian, but rather the transition from the bare profession of Christianity, or 'carnal hypocrisy' to saving faith.[21] Puritans had a variety of ways of distinguishing converted Christians from hypocrites—'the saints,' 'the people of God,' 'the godly,' 'the people of the covenant'—but the way they used the word 'Christian' did not have this restricted and particular quality about it. Its use to embrace both saints and hypocrites reflected the religious character of a society which was still very much shaped by the Christendom paradigm of being church.

Conversion as Process

This is important, not just as an example of changing English usage, but because of the way the prevailing Christendom paradigm shaped Puritan thinking about conversion. In a situation in which almost everyone already thought of themselves as Christians (and therefore as believers), conversion

---

20 For example, the title of Giles Firmin's 1657 work, *The Real Christian.*

was seldom experienced as a sudden and total reversal of spiritual align-ment. Damascus Road experiences were rare. Most of the divines who wrote about the subject were themselves brought up in what we would describe today as 'Christian homes.' Many were second or third generation Puritans; in some cases they were children of clergy. Much of this can be said, too, of many of those to whom they preached and for whom they wrote. Inevitably, for people from such a background, conversion was most often experienced as a gradual process, beginning with stirrings of conscience and leading through remorse, attendance on the means of grace, and contrition (which could be both severe and prolonged) to an ultimate sense of acceptance and peace. It is not helpful, therefore, to bring to Puritan thinking about conver-sion the modern notion of a 'moment' at which the transition between sin and redemption takes place. Puritans were not much concerned about mo-ments; their interest lay in solid evidences of grace collected over protracted periods, not in unverified claims about momentary experiences uncritically received. They would certainly have regarded much modern evangelistic preaching and 'counselling' as hopelessly inadequate, setting the criteria of saving faith at far too much of a discount. Many whom we confidently count as Christians today, because of their reported experience of having turned to God, they would have regarded with deep suspicion as carnal hypocrites on the evidence of their life and conduct.

The emphasis on conversion as process had a second important effect on Puritan conversion literature. As we have seen, much Puritan literature had a homiletic origin; virtually all of it was influenced by the predominance of the sermon as the characteristic literary form of the movement, and this is particularly true of the extensive literature on conversion. Most of this writ-ing, therefore, comprises not theoretical studies of the psychology of the con-version experience, nor even doctrinal treatises on regeneration or the place of conversion in the *ordo salutis*, but homiletic material designed to urge the hearers of sermons to avail themselves of the means of grace, and repent while there is still time. Where commentators have failed adequately to take account of the homiletic literary type in analysing the Puritan theory of con-version, they have been prone to misunderstandings about its underlying theological structure. For instance, R T Kendall has helpfully identified a shift in the way the nature of faith was understood between Calvin, who saw it as a persuasion or conviction that Christ died for one, and William Perkins, who followed Beza in seeing faith as an act of the will exercised in trust or commitment.[22] Kendall rightly points out that Perkins' view of faith

---

2 1 Thus, for example, even as late as 1676, in *The Pilgrim's Progress*, Bunyan significantly names his chief characters 'Christian' and 'Christiana' from the outset, even before they experience any kind of spiritual awakening.
2 2 R T Kendall, *Calvin and English Calvinism to 1649* (Oxford, 1979).

lends itself much more readily than Calvin's to the notion of conversion as a process with faith as its culmination. It is not surprising, therefore, to find Perkins identifying two parts to this process: *preparation*, in which the Law and the conscience make a man ready for grace; and *composition*, which is the inward movement of the Spirit following on from preparation, resulting in true repentance, faith and obedience. Preparation could be a prolonged and painful experience, involving a growing awareness of and conviction of sin, and a series of attempts to deal with the resulting burden of guilt through acts of contrition which, not being rooted in true saving faith, inevitably fail. Contrition of this kind was not the same thing as 'repentance,' a term which was usually reserved for that turning away from sin which accompanied saving faith, both at the time of and after conversion. Kendall traces the Puritan concern with preparation for grace through a series of early seventeenth-century Puritan writers culminating with Thomas Hooker. He argues that voluntaristic preparation becomes more and more explicit and more and more complex in the literature until Hooker reaches the point of suggesting that man 'initiates the process of preparation by making use of the means of grace,' which amounts to a pelagian or Arminian doctrine of conversion.

But unfortunately Kendall nowhere addresses the question of the nature of the Puritan literature. Instead he approaches treatises which obviously originated in the pulpit, and which were published to secure the same ends as the original sermons on which they were based (that is, the repentance and conversion of their readers), as though they were dogmatic and didactic treatises designed to present a judicious and balanced account of the theory of the conversion process. This is inappropriate. The Puritan sermon was not a closely reasoned attempt to present a theologically balanced and rounded account of a theoretical position. It was a means of grace, intended to move its hearers to an appropriate response, and it was designed and constructed to achieve that end as effectively as possible. The fact that Puritan sermons on conversion, and their derivative literature, exhort their hearers or readers to engage in the process of preparation and repentance without, at the same time, telling them that they cannot do so without the transforming power of the Spirit, is not evidence of pelagianism or crypto-synergism. It merely reflects the homiletic context. Puritan preachers exhorted people to repent and believe because they observed that it was when they did so that they experienced conversion. Responding to the invitation was the way in which the means of grace worked, and individuals entered the conversion process. They also believed that no particular person could repent without the enabling power of the Spirit, but to tell them this at the same time as issuing the invitation was both unnecessary and psychologically counterproductive. If they did repent and believe in response to the invitation, well then, that proved that the Spirit was enabling them. If they did not, it was a clear demonstration that the Spirit was not. There was no need to unpack the Spirit's involvement at the same time as issuing the invitation, for the sermon was meant to achieve its end, and it was preached in such a way as to secure that end in the context of the concrete circumstances and actual problems that people consciously experienced in responding to God's grace.

Preparation for Conversion

In view of the effects of the homiletic character of the literature, it is not surprising that Puritans often failed to distinguish between conversion and regeneration. The term 'regeneration' could be used as a description of the whole process of conversion, including preparation for it, or as a simple alternative to conversion more narrowly understood as the part of the process that followed preparation. Equally, however, it could be used to describe the theological phenomenon which underlay the psychological experience of conversion, the one being a work of divine grace, the other an experience of the human affections. Puritans, of course, would not have put the distinction in terms which reflect this post-Enlightenment, 'scientific' understanding of the way human personality functions. Thinking of this sort was simply not available to them; 'psychology' was not part of their vocabulary. Nevertheless, their concern for 'practical, affectionate divinity' sometimes led them in the direction of an implicit distinction along these lines. Thus Richard Sibbes, for instance, speaks of 'the least sign of regeneration' as 'a sign of regeneration begun,' while William Perkins suggests that 'desire for faith' is, in fact, the 'beginnings of faith.' On the whole, however, the Puritans' inability to make an explicit distinction between the theological phenomenon of regeneration and the psychological experience of conversion left them with difficulties over the question of preparation. They had to explain how it was possible for an unregenerate person to enter into a process which would lead to conversion and saving faith, without recourse to the idea of a hidden work of regeneration commencing beforehand and initiating it. Divines, therefore, sought a variety of theological contexts through which to account for the phenomenon of preparation for grace. Some saw it as the outworking of the covenant obligations of baptism, others as a provision of Providence or common grace. All were, however, agreed that preparations for conversion were not meritorious, and that God, rather than man, was their author.

Preparation was necessary because, as Richard Sibbes put it,

'There is such a distance between the nature and corruption of man and grace that there must be a great deal of preparation, many degrees to rise by, before a man come to that condition that he should be in.'[23]

---

23 R Sibbes, 'Lydia's Conversion,' *The Riches of Mercie* (1638) in *Works* (1863) vol VI, p 522.

But he is quick to add the rider that all preparations are from God, and that human beings cannot prepare themselves, or deserve grace through making preparations, for,

> '...there is no force of a meritorious cause in preparations to grace, to raise up the soul to grace; for alas! that cannot be...Yet notwithstanding it brings a man to less distance than other wild creatures that come not within the compass of the means.'[24]

Preparation, therefore, is that part of the process of conversion which takes place as a result of the activity of God but which, being undertaken by an unregenerate person, does not lead with any necessity to the experience of conversion/regeneration for which it is, nevertheless, a preparation! Sibbes solves the implicit tension here through a classic appeal to the providential appointment of means:

> 'The sweet providence of God brings those that belong to election under the compass of the means at one time or another. Let the devil and the instruments of the devil...do what they can, those that belong to God, God will have a time to...effectually call them by his Spirit.'[25]

But is this a solution? If preparation is a result of an effectual call, and only God can initiate it, is it not, in reality, the beginning of regeneration?

As to what was involved in preparation,

> 'Now God, in preparation, for the most part civiliseth people, and then Christianiseth them, as I may say...to break them from their natural rudeness and fierceness...and then, seeing what their estate is in the corruption of nature, to deject them, and then to bring them to Christianity...'[26]

Thus preparation is a process by which a person is brought from wild, unrestrained autonomy to a measure of self-discipline and reason, sufficient for the understanding to begin to attend to the message conveyed by the means. In effect, Sibbes is arguing that it is a movement towards the recovery of the damaged image of God, and the language he uses of it includes the idea of becoming truly human. It involves experiencing conviction of sin, awareness of a burden of guilt, and a desire to have one's conscience cleansed and relieved. It is complete when

---

24 *ibid*, pp 522-3.
25 *ibid*, p 523.
26 *ibid*, p 522.

'...the soul is so far cast down as it sets a high price on Christ and on grace, above all things in the world. It accounts grace the only pearl, and the gospel to be the kingdom of heaven. When a man sets a high price on grace more than all the world besides, then a man is sufficiently pre-pared.'[27]

To set the effect of preparation so high is inevitably to invite the question whether it is possible to set so high a price on grace without grace!

Conversion, Faith and Assurance

Where Calvin construed saving faith as an assurance on the part of a Christian that he or she participated effectually in the salvific consequences of the death and resurrection of Jesus, most Puritans understood faith in more transactional terms. Faith was the act of will by which, in a memorable phrase of Richard Sibbes, someone 'rolled their whole soul on Christ' for salvation. This faith-transaction was not without an element of assurance; 'rolling the soul on Christ' was seen as a consequence of being sure about the objective truth of those historical facts that are the object of faith—Christ's death for sinners and his resurrection for their justification—but most Puri-tans were careful to distinguish faith from assurance as two separate stages in the experience of redemption. On the whole Puritans did not expect that conversion would necessarily, or even normally, lead immediately to assur-ance. Even late in his life Richard Baxter would only admit to being 'toler-ably certain' of his own salvation! Assurance was, after all, a manifestation of strong, mature faith whereas, as we have seen, the conversion process could be said to have begun when the least evidence of saving faith was manifested. Richard Rogers, for instance, could draw attention to the diffi-culty that many Christians had in recognizing their own conversion because the work of the Spirit is so subtle and secret, and their own fears that no change might have occurred could blind them to the evidences of the Spir-it's activity.

One consequence of this was that Puritan pastors were not unduly dis-turbed when confronted by Christians who were uncertain about their spir-itual condition. It was not unusual for the 'saints and people of God' to experience 'humblings' of various kinds—doubts and uncertainties, spir-itual drought, attacks of temptation and spiritual depression or even extended periods in which they were 'deserted' by the Spirit. The literature reflects the pastoral concern to address these experiences,[28] and Puritan 'physicians of the soul' were well versed in techniques and arguments (always, of course, addressed to the understanding) to help Christians discover evidences of

---

27 *ibid*, p 522.
28 One of the better known and most affecting works of this kind is William Bridge, *A Lifting up for the Downcast* (1648) reprinted by the Banner of Truth Trust in paperback in 1961.

saving faith.[29] At the same time, however, it is hard to escape the conclusion that they were themselves at least partially responsible for the high levels of spiritual uncertainty and stress that many of their followers experienced, because of their awareness that not all who claimed saving faith actually had it. There were plenty of examples in their congregations of people who experienced the inward movements of preparation for grace, but who never went on to saving faith, and this problem of counterfeit or 'temporary' faith led some preachers to exercise considerable caution in encouraging would-be believers to feel secure in that stage of the process of experiencing grace they had reached, even if this showed all the signs of conversion completed. William Perkins, for instance, could go so far in describing what was possible in the way of evidences for those who had only temporary faith that little seemed to be left to distinguish true believers from hypocrites. Writing of those who preach to people experiencing 'humiliations' he warns that:

'...here we must diligently consider whether their humiliation be complete and sound, or but begun and but light or slight: lest that he or they, receiving comfort sooner than is meet, should afterwards wax more hard; like iron which being cast into the furnace becomes exceeding hard after that it is once cold.'[30]

And, in another place:

'The promise alone must not be applied, but withal mention must be made of the sinnes of the partie, and of the grievous punishments due unto him for the same...because there is much guile in the heart of man; in so much as oftentime it falleth out that men not thoroughly humbled, being comforted either too soone or too much, doe afterward become the worst of all...The sweetness of comfort is greater if it bee delaied with some tartnesse of the law.'[31]

This concern to set saving faith as high as possible in order to 'fence' it against the self-deluded claims of carnal hypocrites sits uncomfortably with that other strand in Perkins' pastoral theology (which we noted above) that seeks to set it as low as possible so as not to exclude any true subject of the Spirit's work. Moreover, its effect could be devastating. Perhaps the most telling

---

2 9 Thus, for instance, the anonymous writer of *Samuel Hieron's Farewell*, a funeral sermon from 1618, puts these words into the mouth of his subject: '...and seeing that the Fighters bee faithfull and faithfull fighters; it may make much for the comfort of such as have opposition within them, or without them; for truly this is a sure signe that thou art a souldier...the more that thou art tempted by the Devill, the more cause thou hast to gather comfort.'

3 0 W Perkins, *The Arte of Prophesying* (1592) in *Workes II* (1609) p 754.

3 1 W Perkins, *The Whole Treatise of the Cases of Conscience*, in *Workes II* (1609) p 29.

commentary on it is John Bunyan's description of his spiritual roller-coaster ride to an assured faith in *Grace Abounding to the Chief of Sinners*. It is hard to escape the impression, following Bunyan through the tortured maze of his path to spiritual peace, that, in his case at least, regeneration took place long before he was satisfied with his own experience of conversion. Richard Baxter's story, though less extreme, is similar.[32] These and many other instances illustrate the problems of propounding an essentially voluntaristic account of faith, with its correspondingly associational view of church membership, in the context of a Christendom paradigm of faith and practice.

It is, however, the less rigoristic model of saving faith and conversion which represents the more authentic voice of English Puritanism. A whole school of Puritan divines, headed by figures like Richard Sibbes, Robert Bolton and Thomas Hooker, majored on the themes of comfort, consolation and encouragement for doubting Christians.[33] For these writers, experiences of 'humiliation' were opportunities, not so much to turn the screw of the law so as to maximize the spiritual *angst* of the hypocrite, as to apply the poultice of the gospel to wounded spirits, to support bruised reeds and gently to blow the smoking flax to life. Thus Bolton, one of whose favourite texts was Job 13.15, ('though he slay me, yet will I trust in him'), attempted to help believers understand the experience of desertion by a metaphor from family life:

'A father solacing himselfe with his little child and delighting in its pretty and pleasing behaviour is wont, sometimes, to step aside into a corner, or behind a dore, upon purpose to quicken yet more its love and longing after him, and try the impatiency and eagerness of its affection...Conceive then, and consider to thine owne exceeding comfort, that thy heavenly Father deales just so with thee in a spiritual desertion. He sometimes hides his face from thee...to put more heat and life into thine affections towards him and heavenly things.'[34]

It is in the tradition of 'practical affectionate divinity' and 'painful preaching' represented by Bolton's clear concern for the spiritual well-being of individual believers that English Puritanism finds its most enduring qualities. And it is in these traditions of pastoral care and spiritual nurture that succeeding generations are most likely to discover models of good practice for emulation in their own work of spiritual nurture and cure.

---

32 N H Keeble, ed, *The Autobiography of Richard Baxter* (1974), (abridged by J M Lloyd Thomas from *Reliquiae Baxterianae*, 1696) pp 7-11.
33 Richard Sibbes, author of *The Bruised Reed and Smoking Flax* (1630) and *The Returning Backslider* (1639) for instance, was known as 'The Sweet Dropper' because of his tender way with despairing Christians.
34 R Bolton, *Instructions for a Right Comforting Afflicted Consciences* (1631) p 366.

5
What can we Learn from Puritanism?

Can We Learn from the Past at All?

Does Puritanism have anything to offer to Christians on the threshold of the third millennium? It would be easy to say 'no.' It is clear that learning from the past is not easy. It may even be impossible. The context is so different, the world has moved on, issues which have a superficial similarity turn out, on closer inspection, to have radically different antecedents.

A Puritan who found himself transported through time to an Anglican church in Britain today would have a hard time making sense of things. The ways in which modern Anglicans, especially evangelical ones, orientate themselves in relation to the four points of the ecclesiastical compass by which Puritans steered in the seventeenth century—rejecting the use of the sign of the cross in baptism, the ring in marriage, the wearing of surplices and the receiving of Holy Communion kneeling—would all tell him he was in an unreformed church. Much of what goes on in worship today would probably fill him with horror, particularly in relation to music, vestments, church furnishings and decorations and the generally consumerist culture. Contemporary Christians have problems enough with post-modernism; our notional Puritan would find the whole concept of scepticism about meta-narrative utterly incomprehensible. He would quickly reach the conclusion that twentieth century Christians did not share his conviction that all grace is mediated through the understanding. He would probably decide they did not subscribe, either, to his belief that God works ordinarily through means. He would, almost certainly, find the preaching deeply unsatisfactory and superficial, and the attitudes of both clergy and church members hopelessly lacking in precision and method.

Shifting Ecclesiology

The twentieth century is not the seventeenth, and the presuppositions and expectations of the seventeenth century cannot simply be lifted lock, stock and barrel into the present. In particular, the church today is in the throes of a paradigm shift which involves a transition from the Christendom mode of being church familiar to the Puritans to something quite different and much more open. Inasmuch as Puritanism was an implementation of Christendom ecclesiology, it represents part of what we are leaving behind, rather than part of what we are reaching out to. Puritan methodology, with its reliance on scholastic modes of reasoning, its innate conservatism, and its instinctive appeal to meta-narrative and authority, sits less and less comfortably with our increasingly post-modern context.

Abiding Values

Yet as we penetrate, from our twentieth-century standpoint, behind the stereotypes, the world-view, and the historically conditioned context of the seventeenth century, we still encounter in Puritanism something abidingly authentic about Christian experience and ministry. There are themes here that have played a profound part in shaping what we are as Christians today, especially if our cultural roots are anglo-saxon and our spiritual identity has been defined, at least in part, by evangelicalism. In an age of instant tell, instant reaction, instant experience, where the waiting has long been taken out of wanting, the Puritan understanding of conversion as process, and the commitment to 'painful' preaching and spiritual nurture, not only speak of a more spacious age but invite us to look more deeply beneath the surface of our own experience and that of those whom we seek to bring to faith and discipleship in our churches. We are much more likely on the threshold of the third millennium, than they were in the middle of the second, to find ourselves dealing with a post-christendom pattern of sudden conversion experience in which it may be the Philippian gaoler rather than Lydia, the God-fearing seller of purple, who offers us the most apposite model. But that does not afford us excuses for taking refuge in over-simplifications of God's ways with his people, or failing to understand the capacity of the human heart for self-deception.

Christian Maturity

Above all, what is compelling about the Puritan tradition we have been considering here is its concern for victims—the bruised reeds and 'poore doubting Christians' who were the subjects of the spiritual physic administered by the spiritual doctors. What lay behind that programme of care and nurture was the aim of presenting each Christian mature in Christ, freed from the debilitating burdens of doubt and guilt and able, at least in measure, to take responsibility for their own relationship with God and its sustenance through the right use of the means of grace.

It is the case, of course, that Puritan pastors, like twentieth-century clergy, were not always completely true to that aim. Like some clergy in every generation, including our own, they were not above paternalism, and a tendency to magnify the pastoral office so as to retain a significant hold over the members of their flocks through the promotion of a culture of dependency. There was an inescapable clericalism in their approach to spiritual nurture which is mirrored in the role of some clergy in the local church today, even in those sections of the church in which the rhetoric of every-member ministry and collaborative responsibility for leadership is most evident. But the aim of liberating Christian believers into mature and responsible discipleship is evidently implicit in the whole approach of Puritan spirituality. The language and methodology the Puritans used may have belonged to the seventeenth century, but the objective is one which challenges the church today as much as it did then. Programmes of spiritual development which enforce fear and engender dependence in the end serve only the vested interests of the ecclesially powerful. What the saints and people of God need today, as in the Puritan era, is to be set free to know God for themselves, and to glorify and enjoy him for ever.

Further Reading

There is a vast literature on all aspects of English Puritanism. The following is a selection of classic introductions, together with some of the texts which specifically address questions of Puritan spirituality.

Basic Introductions to English Puritanism

P Collinson, *The Elizabethan Puritan Movement* (Jonathan Cape, 1967)
G R Cragg, *Puritanism in the Period of the Great Persecution* (CUP, 1957)
W Haller, *The Rise of Puritanism* (Harper, 1957)
P Miller, *The New England Mind, vol 1: The Seventeenth Century* (Beacon, 1961)
M R Watts, *The Dissenters* (OUP, 1978)

Texts on Puritan Spirituality

J S Coolidge, *The Pauline Renaissance in England* (OUP, 1970)
R T Kendall, *Calvin and English Calvinism to 1649* (OUP, 1979)
P Lewis, *The Genius of Puritanism* (Carey, 1975)
J Sears McGee, *The Godly Man in Stuart England* (Yale UP, 1976)
I Morgan, *Puritan Spirituality* (Epworth, 1973)
G F Nuttall, *The Holy Spirit in Puritan Faith and Experience* (OUP, 1947)
N Pettit, *The Heart Prepared* (Yale UP, 1966)
O C Watkins, *The Puritan Experience* (Routledge & Kegan Paul, 1972)

Puritan Texts

In the end there is no substitute for reading the Puritans themselves. However, this can seem a daunting task to those unfamiliar with seventeenth-century theological literature. Here are some suggestions about where to start, most of which are modern paperback reprints.

Thomas Brooks, *Heaven on Earth* (Banner of Truth, 1961)
Thomas Brooks, *Precious Remedies Against Satan's Devices* (Banner of Truth, 1968)
Jeremiah Burroughes, *The Rare Jewel of Christian Contentment* (Banner of Truth, 1964)
William Bridge, *A Lifting up for the Downcast* (Banner of Truth, 1961)
Richard Sibbes, 'The Bruised Reed and Smoking Flax,' in *Complete Works, vol 1* (Nichol, 1862)